Living a Life of Purpose: Discovering God's Plan for Your Life

Dorothy Vincent

Published by RWG Publishing, 2023.

While every precaution has been taken in the preparation of this book, the publisher assumes no responsibility for errors or omissions, or for damages resulting from the use of the information contained herein.

LIVING A LIFE OF PURPOSE: DISCOVERING GOD'S PLAN FOR YOUR LIFE

First edition. March 28, 2023.

Copyright © 2023 Dorothy Vincent.

Written by Dorothy Vincent.

Also by Dorothy Vincent

The Case of the Missing Heirloom: A Whodunit Mystery
The Lost City of Atlantis: A Young Adult Adventure
Living Authentically: Embracing Your Unique Identity
The Faithful Witness: Conviction and Courage in Uncertain Times
Breaking the Mold: Shattering Expectations and Chasing Dreams
The Art of Being Yourself: Uncovering the Power of Authenticity
Living a Life of Purpose: Discovering God's Plan for Your Life

Table of Contents

Chapter 1: Introduction - The Importance of Living a Life of Purpose...........1
Chapter 2: What is God's Plan for Your Life?...........3
Chapter 3: The Benefits of Living a Life of Purpose...........5
Chapter 4: Understanding Your Identity in Christ...........7
Chapter 5: Discovering Your Spiritual Gifts...........9
Chapter 6: Finding Your Passion and Purpose...........11
Chapter 7: Developing a Vision for Your Life...........13
Chapter 8: Overcoming Fear and Doubt in Pursuing Your Purpose...........15
Chapter 9: The Role of Prayer in Discovering Your Purpose...........17
Chapter 10: Understanding God's Timing for Your Life...........19
Chapter 11: Dealing with Setbacks and Obstacles...........21
Chapter 12: Trusting God's Guidance on Your Life Journey...........23
Chapter 13: Living with Courage and Conviction...........25
Chapter 14: The Power of Gratitude in Living a Purposeful Life...........27
Chapter 15: Living a Life of Service to Others...........29
Chapter 16: The Importance of Rest and Self-Care in Pursuing Your Purpose...........31
Chapter 17: The Role of Faith in Living a Life of Purpose...........33
Chapter 18: Navigating Relationships and Community in Pursuing Your Purpose...........35
Chapter 19: The Role of Perseverance in Achieving Your Purpose...........37
Chapter 20: Discovering Your Life's Mission and Calling...........39
Chapter 21: The Importance of Character in Living a Purposeful Life...........41
Chapter 22: Overcoming Distractions and Staying Focused on Your Purpose...........43
Chapter 23: Building a Support System for Pursuing Your Purpose...........45

Chapter 24: Embracing Change and Adaptability on Your Life Journey 47

Chapter 25: Learning from Failures and Mistakes on Your Purposeful Path 49

Chapter 26: Aligning Your Goals with God's Purpose for Your Life 51

Chapter 27: The Role of Wisdom in Living a Purposeful Life 53

Chapter 28: Building a Legacy of Purpose and Impact 55

Chapter 29: Living with Joy and Purpose in Every Season of Life 57

Chapter 30: Conclusion - Embracing God's Plan for Your Life 59

Chapter 1: Introduction - The Importance of Living a Life of Purpose

Living a life of purpose is one of the most fulfilling and rewarding experiences one can have. It is a journey that involves self-discovery, self-awareness, and self-actualization. Many people today struggle with finding meaning and direction in their lives, which often leads to feelings of frustration, hopelessness, and despair. Living a life of purpose is essential to our well-being, as it helps us to make sense of our existence and provides us with a sense of direction and meaning.

The first step towards living a life of purpose is to understand what it means. Simply put, living a life of purpose means aligning your thoughts, beliefs, and actions with a higher calling or a greater cause. It involves recognizing and fulfilling your unique role in the world and using your talents, skills, and abilities to make a positive impact on others. This can be achieved through various means such as pursuing a career that aligns with your passions, serving others through volunteering or community work, or simply living a life of integrity and kindness.

Living a life of purpose has numerous benefits. It can lead to greater happiness and fulfillment, increased resilience, and improved mental and physical health. Studies have shown that people who live a life of purpose have a lower risk of developing chronic illnesses, such as heart disease and stroke, and are more likely to experience greater levels of satisfaction and contentment in life. In addition, people who live a life of purpose are more resilient and better equipped to cope with setbacks and challenges, as they have a sense of direction and meaning to guide them.

However, living a life of purpose is not always easy. It requires commitment, perseverance, and a willingness to step outside of your comfort zone. It also involves facing your fears and insecurities, and taking risks to pursue your dreams and aspirations. Despite these challenges, living a life of purpose is a journey that is well worth taking. It is an opportunity to live a life of significance and impact, and to make a positive difference in the world.

In this book, we will explore the various aspects of living a life of purpose, including understanding God's plan for your life, discovering your spiritual gifts, finding your passion and purpose, and overcoming fear and doubt in pursuing your purpose. We will also discuss the importance of prayer, faith, and community in living a purposeful life, as well as the role of character, wisdom, and perseverance in achieving your purpose.

Whether you are just beginning your journey towards living a life of purpose or have been on this path for some time, this book will provide you with valuable insights, practical tips, and inspiring stories to guide and encourage you along the way. So, let us begin this journey together, as we explore what it means to live a life of purpose and discover God's plan for our lives.

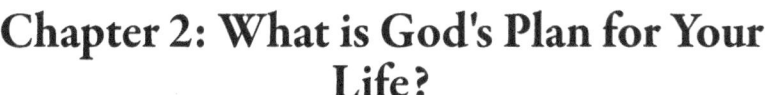

Chapter 2: What is God's Plan for Your Life?

One of the most fundamental questions we can ask ourselves is, "What is God's plan for my life?" This question reflects a desire to understand our purpose, our place in the world, and our relationship with God. Discovering God's plan for our lives requires us to look beyond our own desires and ambitions and seek God's will for us.

The Bible teaches us that God has a plan for each of us. In Jeremiah 29:11, God says, "For I know the plans I have for you, plans to prosper you and not to harm you, plans to give you hope and a future." This verse reminds us that God has a purpose and a plan for our lives that is good and beneficial for us. God's plan for our lives is unique to each of us, as we are all created with different gifts, talents, and abilities.

To discover God's plan for our lives, we must first seek God's guidance. This involves spending time in prayer, reading the Bible, and seeking the counsel of wise and trusted advisors. Through prayer and reading the Bible, we can discern God's will for our lives and gain a deeper understanding of His plan for us. Seeking the counsel of others can also provide valuable insights and perspectives that can help us to better understand God's plan for our lives.

Another important aspect of discovering God's plan for our lives is surrendering our own will and desires to God. This means letting go of our own ambitions and trusting that God's plan for us is better than anything we could ever imagine. Surrendering to God's will requires humility, faith, and a willingness to let go of control. It also involves accepting God's timing, even when it doesn't align with our own.

Discovering God's plan for our lives also involves understanding and using our gifts and talents to serve others. God has given each of us unique abilities that can be used to make a positive impact on the world. By using our gifts and talents to serve others, we can fulfill our purpose and bring glory to God.

Living according to God's plan for our lives also requires obedience. Obedience to God means putting His will above our own and following His guidance, even when it goes against our own desires or preferences. Obedience to God requires trust, faith, and a willingness to obey even when we don't fully understand His plan for us.

In conclusion, discovering God's plan for our lives is a lifelong journey that requires prayer, seeking guidance, surrender, using our gifts to serve others, and obedience to God. God's plan for our lives is unique to each of us and is designed to bring glory to Him and benefit to us. By seeking God's plan for our lives and aligning our will with His, we can live a purposeful and fulfilling life.

Chapter 3: The Benefits of Living a Life of Purpose

Living a life of purpose is not only essential for our spiritual growth, but it also has numerous benefits for our mental, emotional, and physical well-being. In this chapter, we will explore some of the benefits of living a life of purpose and how it can positively impact various aspects of our lives.

Increased Happiness and Fulfillment: Living a life of purpose gives us a sense of direction and meaning. It allows us to feel like we are making a difference in the world and living up to our potential. This sense of fulfillment and purpose can lead to greater happiness and contentment in life.

Improved Mental Health: Living a life of purpose can have a positive impact on our mental health. Studies have shown that people who have a sense of purpose have a lower risk of developing depression, anxiety, and other mental health disorders. Living a life of purpose also helps us to better cope with stress and adversity.

Better Physical Health: Living a life of purpose can also have a positive impact on our physical health. People who live a life of purpose have been shown to have a lower risk of developing chronic diseases such as heart disease, stroke, and diabetes. They are also more likely to engage in healthy behaviors such as exercise and healthy eating.

Increased Resilience: Living a life of purpose helps us to better cope with challenges and setbacks. It gives us a sense of direction and meaning that helps us to stay focused and motivated, even in difficult times. This increased resilience can help us to overcome obstacles and achieve our goals.

Stronger Relationships: Living a life of purpose can also have a positive impact on our relationships. When we are living according to our purpose, we are more likely to attract people who share our values and beliefs. We are also more likely to have fulfilling relationships, as we are more likely to be focused on giving and serving others.

Greater Sense of Community: Living a life of purpose can also lead to a greater sense of community. When we are living according to our purpose, we are more likely to be involved in activities and organizations that align with our values and beliefs. This can lead to a sense of belonging and connection with others who share our passions and interests.

Increased Self-Awareness: Living a life of purpose requires us to be self-aware and introspective. We must understand our strengths, weaknesses, and motivations in order to fulfill our purpose. This increased self-awareness can lead to greater personal growth and development.

Legacy Building: Living a life of purpose allows us to leave a positive impact on the world. When we are living according to our purpose, we are more likely to make a difference in the lives of others and leave a lasting legacy.

In conclusion, living a life of purpose has numerous benefits for our mental, emotional, and physical well-being. It gives us a sense of direction and meaning, helps us to cope with challenges and setbacks, and allows us to leave a positive impact on the world. By living a life of purpose, we can experience greater happiness, fulfillment, and personal growth.

Chapter 4: Understanding Your Identity in Christ

Understanding your identity in Christ is an essential aspect of living a life of purpose. Our identity in Christ is not based on our accomplishments, possessions, or social status, but rather on who we are in Christ. In this chapter, we will explore what it means to have our identity in Christ and how it can impact our lives.

Our identity in Christ is rooted in the fact that we are children of God. When we accept Jesus Christ as our Lord and Savior, we become part of the family of God. As Romans 8:16-17 says, "The Spirit himself testifies with our spirit that we are God's children. Now if we are children, then we are heirs—heirs of God and co-heirs with Christ." This means that our identity is not based on our own merits or accomplishments, but rather on the fact that we are part of God's family.

Understanding our identity in Christ means understanding that we are loved, valued, and accepted by God. As Ephesians 1:4-5 says, "For he chose us in him before the creation of the world to be holy and blameless in his sight. In love he predestined us for adoption to sonship through Jesus Christ, in accordance with his pleasure and will." This means that our worth and value are not based on what we do or achieve, but rather on the fact that we are chosen and loved by God.

Understanding our identity in Christ also means understanding that we have been redeemed and forgiven through the sacrifice of Jesus Christ. As 1 Peter 2:9-10 says, "But you are a chosen people, a royal priesthood, a holy nation, God's special possession, that you may declare the praises of him who called you out of darkness into his wonderful light. Once you were not a people, but now you are the people of God; once you had not received mercy, but now you have received mercy." This means that our past mistakes and failures do not define us, but rather we are defined by our relationship with God.

Understanding our identity in Christ can have a profound impact on our lives. It gives us a sense of purpose and meaning that is not based on our own accomplishments or possessions, but rather on who we are in Christ. It also gives us a sense of security and confidence, as we know that we are loved and valued by God. Understanding our identity in Christ can also help us to overcome feelings of inadequacy, low self-esteem, and self-doubt.

Living according to our identity in Christ means living a life of faith, obedience, and service to God. It means seeking to live a life that is pleasing to God, and using our gifts and talents to serve others. It also means seeking to align our will with God's will, even when it goes against our own desires or preferences.

In conclusion, understanding our identity in Christ is essential to living a life of purpose. It means recognizing that our worth and value are not based on what we do or achieve, but rather on who we are in Christ. It also means living a life of faith, obedience, and service to God. By understanding our identity in Christ, we can live a life of purpose and meaning that is grounded in our relationship with God.

Chapter 5: Discovering Your Spiritual Gifts

As believers, each one of us has been given spiritual gifts by God. These gifts are designed to help us fulfill our purpose and serve others. In this chapter, we will explore what spiritual gifts are, how to discover them, and how to use them to live a life of purpose.

Spiritual gifts are special abilities that are given to us by the Holy Spirit. These gifts are not natural talents or skills, but rather supernatural abilities that are given to us for the purpose of serving God and others. As 1 Corinthians 12:4-6 says, "There are different kinds of gifts, but the same Spirit distributes them. There are different kinds of service, but the same Lord. There are different kinds of working, but in all of them and in everyone it is the same God at work."

There are many different spiritual gifts that are listed in the Bible, such as the gift of prophecy, the gift of wisdom, the gift of healing, the gift of faith, and many others. Each of these gifts is given to us by the Holy Spirit for a specific purpose, and they are intended to be used to build up the body of Christ.

Discovering your spiritual gifts involves prayer, self-reflection, and seeking the guidance of others. Here are some steps you can take to discover your spiritual gifts:

Pray: Ask God to reveal your spiritual gifts to you. Spend time in prayer and ask the Holy Spirit to show you how you can use your gifts to serve others.

Self-reflection: Think about the things you enjoy doing and are good at. Consider how you can use these skills and abilities to serve others and glorify God.

Seek the guidance of others: Ask trusted friends, family members, or church leaders for their insights and perspectives on your gifts and how they might be used to serve others.

Once you have discovered your spiritual gifts, it is important to use them to serve others. As 1 Peter 4:10-11 says, "Each of you should use whatever gift you have received to serve others, as faithful stewards of God's grace in its various forms. If anyone speaks, they should do so as one who speaks the very words of God. If anyone serves, they should do so with the strength God provides, so that in all things God may be praised through Jesus Christ."

Using our spiritual gifts to serve others allows us to live a life of purpose and meaning. It allows us to make a positive impact on the world and fulfill our role in the body of Christ. It also allows us to experience the joy and satisfaction that comes from serving others and using our gifts to bring glory to God.

In conclusion, discovering our spiritual gifts is essential to living a life of purpose. It allows us to understand our unique role in the body of Christ and how we can use our gifts to serve others. By using our spiritual gifts to serve others, we can fulfill our purpose and bring glory to God.

Chapter 6: Finding Your Passion and Purpose

One of the keys to living a life of purpose is to find your passion and purpose. When we are passionate about something, it gives us a sense of direction and meaning. In this chapter, we will explore how to find your passion and purpose, and how to align them with God's plan for your life.

Finding your passion and purpose involves exploring your interests, values, and talents. It also involves understanding how you can use these things to make a positive impact on the world. Here are some steps you can take to find your passion and purpose:

Explore Your Interests: Take some time to reflect on the things that interest you. What do you enjoy doing in your free time? What topics do you enjoy reading about or discussing with others? Consider how you can turn your interests into a career or a way to serve others.

Identify Your Values: Think about the things that are important to you. What values do you hold dear? How can you align your values with your career or your service to others?

Consider Your Talents: Think about the things you are naturally good at. What skills or abilities do you have that could be used to make a positive impact on the world? Consider how you can use your talents to serve others.

Seek Guidance: Ask trusted friends, family members, or church leaders for their insights and perspectives on your interests, values, and talents. They may be able to provide you with valuable insights and guidance on how to find your passion and purpose.

Once you have identified your passion and purpose, it is important to align them with God's plan for your life. This involves seeking God's guidance and understanding how you can use your passions and purpose to serve Him and others. Here are some ways to align your passion and purpose with God's plan for your life:

Seek God's Guidance: Spend time in prayer and ask God to reveal His plan for your life. Seek His guidance on how you can use your passions and purpose to serve Him and others.

Serve Others: Look for opportunities to serve others in ways that align with your passions and purpose. Whether it's volunteering at a local charity, serving in your church, or pursuing a career that aligns with your passions, find ways to use your gifts and talents to make a positive impact on the world.

Seek Accountability: Find an accountability partner or mentor who can help you stay focused on your passions and purpose. They can provide you with encouragement, support, and guidance as you navigate your journey.

In conclusion, finding your passion and purpose is essential to living a life of purpose. It allows you to understand your unique role in the world and how you can use your gifts and talents to make a positive impact on the world. By aligning your passion and purpose with God's plan for your life, you can live a life of purpose and fulfill your role in the body of Christ.

Chapter 7: Developing a Vision for Your Life

Developing a vision for your life is an important step in living a life of purpose. A vision gives you a clear sense of direction and helps you to focus on what is truly important. In this chapter, we will explore how to develop a vision for your life and how to align it with God's plan for your life.

Developing a vision for your life involves setting goals and creating a plan for achieving them. It also involves understanding your priorities and what truly matters to you. Here are some steps you can take to develop a vision for your life:

Set Goals: Identify the things you want to achieve in your life. Write them down and make them specific and measurable. Consider both short-term and long-term goals.

Prioritize: Determine which goals are most important to you and focus on those first. Consider how achieving these goals will impact your life and the lives of others.

Create a Plan: Develop a plan for achieving your goals. Identify the steps you need to take to accomplish each goal and create a timeline for achieving them.

Stay Focused: Stay focused on your vision and your goals. Don't get sidetracked by distractions or setbacks. Keep your vision in mind and stay committed to achieving your goals.

Once you have developed a vision for your life, it is important to align it with God's plan for your life. This involves seeking God's guidance and understanding how your vision fits into His plan for your life. Here are some ways to align your vision with God's plan for your life:

Seek God's Guidance: Spend time in prayer and ask God to reveal His plan for your life. Seek His guidance on how your vision fits into His plan.

Seek Accountability: Find an accountability partner or mentor who can help you stay focused on your vision and hold you accountable to achieving your goals. They can provide you with encouragement, support, and guidance as you navigate your journey.

Serve Others: Look for ways to use your vision and your goals to serve others. Consider how you can make a positive impact on the world and fulfill your role in the body of Christ.

In conclusion, developing a vision for your life is essential to living a life of purpose. It allows you to focus on what is truly important and provides you with a clear sense of direction. By aligning your vision with God's plan for your life, you can live a life of purpose and fulfill your role in the body of Christ.

Chapter 8: Overcoming Fear and Doubt in Pursuing Your Purpose

Pursuing your purpose can be an exciting and fulfilling journey, but it can also be fraught with fear and doubt. Fear and doubt can prevent us from taking risks, pursuing our dreams, and living a life of purpose. In this chapter, we will explore how to overcome fear and doubt and pursue your purpose with confidence.

Identify Your Fears: The first step in overcoming fear and doubt is to identify them. What are you afraid of? What doubts do you have about your ability to pursue your purpose? Write them down and acknowledge them.

Challenge Your Fears: Once you have identified your fears, challenge them. Ask yourself if they are based on reality or if they are simply limiting beliefs. Consider the worst-case scenario and how you would handle it if it were to happen.

Surround Yourself with Support: Surround yourself with people who believe in you and support your goals. Seek out mentors, friends, and family members who can provide you with encouragement and guidance.

Take Small Steps: Overcoming fear and doubt often requires taking small steps. Break down your goals into smaller, manageable tasks and tackle them one at a time. Celebrate your successes along the way, no matter how small they may be.

Focus on Your Strengths: Focus on your strengths and the things you are good at. Consider how you can use your strengths to pursue your purpose and make a positive impact on the world.

Embrace Failure: Understand that failure is a natural part of the journey. Embrace it as an opportunity to learn and grow. Reframe your failures as opportunities for growth and use them as motivation to keep pushing forward.

Practice Self-Care: Taking care of yourself is essential in overcoming fear and doubt. Practice self-care by getting enough rest, exercise, and healthy food. Take breaks when you need them and engage in activities that bring you joy and relaxation.

In conclusion, overcoming fear and doubt is essential to pursuing your purpose with confidence. By identifying your fears, challenging them, surrounding yourself with support, taking small steps, focusing on your strengths, embracing failure, and practicing self-care, you can overcome fear and doubt and pursue your purpose with confidence. Remember that pursuing your purpose is a journey, not a destination, and embrace the challenges and opportunities for growth that come along the way.

Chapter 9: The Role of Prayer in Discovering Your Purpose

Prayer is a powerful tool in discovering and fulfilling your purpose. It allows you to connect with God, seek His guidance, and understand His plan for your life. In this chapter, we will explore the role of prayer in discovering your purpose and how to make prayer a regular part of your journey.

Seek God's Guidance: One of the most important roles of prayer in discovering your purpose is to seek God's guidance. Spend time in prayer and ask God to reveal His plan for your life. Listen to His voice and be open to His direction.

Surrender Your Will: Another important role of prayer in discovering your purpose is to surrender your will to God. Ask Him to guide you and direct your steps. Surrender your own desires and plans to Him and trust in His plan for your life.

Listen to Your Heart: Prayer also allows you to listen to your heart and discern what truly matters to you. As you pray, pay attention to the desires and passions that arise within you. Consider how these desires and passions can be aligned with God's plan for your life.

Find Peace and Clarity: Prayer can also bring you peace and clarity as you navigate your journey. When you are feeling lost or confused, spend time in prayer and ask God to bring you peace and clarity. Allow Him to calm your fears and anxieties and provide you with the clarity you need to move forward.

Practice Gratitude: Finally, prayer allows you to practice gratitude and thankfulness. As you pray, thank God for the gifts and blessings in your life. This attitude of gratitude can help you to stay focused on what is truly important and appreciate the journey, even in the midst of challenges and difficulties.

Making prayer a regular part of your journey to discovering your purpose is essential. Here are some ways to incorporate prayer into your daily routine:

Set Aside Time: Set aside time each day to spend in prayer. Whether it's in the morning, afternoon, or evening, make prayer a priority and create a routine around it.

Pray Throughout the Day: In addition to setting aside dedicated time for prayer, make an effort to pray throughout the day. Offer up quick prayers of gratitude, guidance, and support as you go about your day.

Use Prayer as a Tool: Use prayer as a tool to help you navigate challenges and difficult situations. When you are feeling lost or confused, turn to prayer for guidance and support.

Pray with Others: Praying with others can be a powerful way to deepen your connection with God and gain insights and perspectives from others. Consider joining a prayer group or seeking out a prayer partner.

In conclusion, prayer is an essential tool in discovering and fulfilling your purpose. By seeking God's guidance, surrendering your will, listening to your heart, finding peace and clarity, and practicing gratitude, you can make prayer a powerful force in your journey to living a life of purpose.

Chapter 10: Understanding God's Timing for Your Life

Understanding God's timing for your life is essential in living a life of purpose. It allows you to trust in His plan, remain patient and faithful, and embrace the journey. In this chapter, we will explore how to understand God's timing for your life and how to trust in His plan.

Trust in God's Plan: One of the most important things you can do to understand God's timing for your life is to trust in His plan. Understand that God's plan is perfect, even if it doesn't always align with your own plans and desires. Trust that He knows what is best for you and that His timing is always perfect.

Seek God's Guidance: Spend time in prayer and seek God's guidance on His timing for your life. Ask Him to reveal His plan and His timing to you. Listen for His voice and be open to His direction.

Embrace the Journey: Embrace the journey and understand that it is a process. God's timing may not always align with your own timeline, but that doesn't mean you are off track. Embrace the journey and the opportunities for growth and learning that come along the way.

Remain Patient and Faithful: Patience and faith are essential in understanding God's timing for your life. Remain patient and faithful, even in the midst of challenges and setbacks. Trust in God's plan and know that His timing is always perfect.

Focus on the Present: Focus on the present moment and what you can do right now to fulfill your purpose. Don't get caught up in worrying about the future or dwelling on the past. Live in the present and focus on what you can do today to make a positive impact on the world.

Stay Flexible: Understand that God's timing may not always align with your own plans and desires. Stay flexible and open to His direction. Be willing to pivot and adjust your plans as necessary.

In conclusion, understanding God's timing for your life is essential in living a life of purpose. By trusting in His plan, seeking His guidance, embracing the journey, remaining patient and faithful, focusing on the present, and staying flexible, you can understand His timing and fulfill your purpose. Remember that God's timing is always perfect, even if it doesn't always align with your own plans and desires. Trust in Him and His plan, and embrace the journey with faith and gratitude.

Chapter 11: Dealing with Setbacks and Obstacles

Setbacks and obstacles are a natural part of the journey to fulfilling your purpose. They can be frustrating, discouraging, and challenging, but they can also provide opportunities for growth and learning. In this chapter, we will explore how to deal with setbacks and obstacles and stay on track towards fulfilling your purpose.

Reframe Your Perspective: One of the most important things you can do when facing setbacks and obstacles is to reframe your perspective. Instead of seeing them as roadblocks, see them as opportunities for growth and learning. Reframe your mindset to focus on what you can learn from the experience and how you can use it to become stronger and more resilient.

Seek Support: Surround yourself with people who can provide you with encouragement and support when facing setbacks and obstacles. Seek out mentors, friends, and family members who can offer guidance, insights, and support.

Stay Positive: Maintaining a positive attitude is essential in dealing with setbacks and obstacles. Focus on the things that are going well in your life and find ways to stay optimistic about the future. Use positive affirmations, visualization, and gratitude practices to stay positive and motivated.

Learn from Your Mistakes: Setbacks and obstacles often provide opportunities for learning and growth. Take the time to reflect on what went wrong and how you can learn from the experience. Use this information to adjust your approach and make changes for the future.

Stay Committed: Staying committed to your purpose and your goals is essential in dealing with setbacks and obstacles. Don't give up on your dreams or let setbacks and obstacles derail you from your path. Stay committed and stay focused on your purpose.

Stay Flexible: Finally, staying flexible is essential in dealing with setbacks and obstacles. Understand that your plans may need to change or adjust as you navigate challenges along the way. Be willing to pivot and adjust your approach as necessary to stay on track towards fulfilling your purpose.

In conclusion, dealing with setbacks and obstacles is an essential part of the journey to fulfilling your purpose. By reframing your perspective, seeking support, staying positive, learning from your mistakes, staying committed, and staying flexible, you can navigate challenges with resilience and stay on track towards your goals. Remember that setbacks and obstacles are opportunities for growth and learning, and use them as motivation to keep pushing forward towards fulfilling your purpose.

Chapter 12: Trusting God's Guidance on Your Life Journey

Trusting God's guidance is essential in living a life of purpose. It allows you to surrender your will to His plan and trust in His perfect timing. In this chapter, we will explore how to trust God's guidance on your life journey and how to make it a regular part of your life.

Seek God's Will: The first step in trusting God's guidance is to seek His will for your life. Spend time in prayer and ask God to reveal His plan for your life. Listen for His voice and be open to His direction.

Surrender Your Will: Once you have discerned God's will, surrender your own will to His plan. Trust that He knows what is best for you and that His plan is perfect. Surrender your own desires and plans to Him and trust in His guidance.

Follow His Direction: As you navigate your journey, follow God's direction. Stay attuned to His guidance and be open to His direction. Trust in His plan, even when it doesn't align with your own plans and desires.

Lean on His Strength: Trusting God's guidance also involves leaning on His strength. When facing challenges and difficulties, turn to God for support and guidance. Draw on His strength and wisdom to navigate the challenges and stay on track towards fulfilling your purpose.

Trust in His Timing: Finally, trusting God's guidance involves trusting in His timing. Understand that His timing may not always align with your own plans and desires. Trust that His timing is always perfect and stay patient and faithful as you wait for His direction.

Making trusting God's guidance a regular part of your life is essential. Here are some ways to incorporate it into your daily routine:

Spend Time in Prayer: Set aside time each day to spend in prayer. Seek God's guidance and surrender your will to His plan.

Read the Bible: The Bible is a powerful source of wisdom and guidance. Spend time each day reading the Bible and reflecting on how its teachings apply to your life.

Surround Yourself with Support: Surround yourself with people who can provide you with encouragement and support as you navigate your journey. Seek out mentors, friends, and family members who can offer guidance and wisdom.

Serve Others: Serving others is an important way to stay connected to God's guidance. Look for ways to use your gifts and talents to serve others and make a positive impact on the world.

In conclusion, trusting God's guidance is essential in living a life of purpose. By seeking God's will, surrendering your own will, following His direction, leaning on His strength, and trusting in His timing, you can navigate your journey with faith and confidence. Remember to make trusting God's guidance a regular part of your life by spending time in prayer, reading the Bible, surrounding yourself with support, and serving others. Trust in His plan and His perfect timing, and embrace the journey with faith and gratitude.

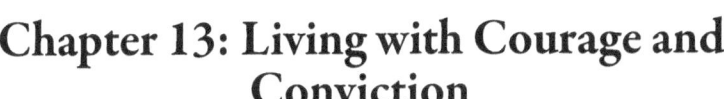

Chapter 13: Living with Courage and Conviction

Living a life of purpose requires courage and conviction. It means standing up for your beliefs and values, even when it's difficult. In this chapter, we will explore how to live with courage and conviction and make a positive impact on the world.

Know Your Values: The first step in living with courage and conviction is to know your values. Identify the things that are most important to you and make them a priority in your life. This will help you to stay grounded in your beliefs and stand up for what you believe in.

Stand Up for Your Beliefs: Living with courage and conviction means standing up for your beliefs, even when it's difficult. Speak up for what you believe in and advocate for the things that matter to you. Don't be afraid to challenge the status quo and make a difference in the world.

Take Calculated Risks: Living with courage and conviction also involves taking calculated risks. Don't be afraid to step outside of your comfort zone and pursue your dreams, even if it means taking risks. Be smart and strategic in your approach, but don't let fear hold you back from pursuing your purpose.

Surround Yourself with Support: Surround yourself with people who believe in you and support your goals. Seek out mentors, friends, and family members who can provide you with encouragement and guidance.

Embrace Failure: Understand that failure is a natural part of the journey. Embrace it as an opportunity to learn and grow. Reframe your failures as opportunities for growth and use them as motivation to keep pushing forward.

Stay True to Yourself: Finally, living with courage and conviction means staying true to yourself. Don't compromise your values or beliefs to fit in or please others. Stay true to yourself and your purpose, and don't be afraid to blaze your own trail.

Incorporating living with courage and conviction into your daily life is essential. Here are some ways to do it:

Set Goals: Set goals that align with your values and purpose. Use these goals to stay focused and motivated.

Practice Self-Care: Taking care of yourself is essential in living with courage and conviction. Practice self-care by getting enough rest, exercise, and healthy food. Take breaks when you need them and engage in activities that bring you joy and relaxation.

Take Action: Living with courage and conviction means taking action. Don't just talk about your beliefs and values, put them into action. Look for opportunities to make a positive impact on the world and take action to make a difference.

Reflect and Evaluate: Take time to reflect on your journey and evaluate your progress. Use this reflection as an opportunity to identify areas for growth and improvement.

In conclusion, living with courage and conviction is essential in fulfilling your purpose and making a positive impact on the world. By knowing your values, standing up for your beliefs, taking calculated risks, surrounding yourself with support, embracing failure, and staying true to yourself, you can live with courage and conviction and make a difference in the world. Remember to incorporate living with courage and conviction into your daily routine by setting goals, practicing self-care, taking action, and reflecting and evaluating your progress. Stay true to your purpose and embrace the journey with faith and courage.

Chapter 14: The Power of Gratitude in Living a Purposeful Life

Gratitude is a powerful tool in living a purposeful life. It allows you to focus on the things that matter most, appreciate the present moment, and find joy in the journey. In this chapter, we will explore the power of gratitude in living a purposeful life and how to incorporate it into your daily routine.

Appreciate the Present Moment: Gratitude allows you to appreciate the present moment and find joy in the journey. Instead of focusing on the things you don't have or the challenges you are facing, focus on the things you do have and the blessings in your life. Take time to appreciate the beauty of the world around you and find joy in the little things.

Focus on What Matters: Gratitude also allows you to focus on the things that matter most. Instead of getting caught up in the busyness of life, take time to reflect on what is truly important to you. Use this reflection to guide your decisions and actions, and make sure that you are living in alignment with your purpose.

Practice Mindfulness: Mindfulness is a powerful tool in cultivating gratitude. By staying present and aware of the moment, you can appreciate the beauty of the world around you and find joy in the little things. Practice mindfulness by staying focused on the present moment and letting go of distractions and worries.

Find Ways to Give Back: Gratitude also involves giving back to others. Look for ways to use your gifts and talents to make a positive impact on the world. Give back to your community, volunteer your time and resources, and find ways to serve others.

Keep a Gratitude Journal: Keeping a gratitude journal is an excellent way to cultivate gratitude in your daily life. Each day, write down a few things that you are grateful for. This practice can help you to stay focused on the blessings in your life and find joy in the journey.

Incorporating gratitude into your daily routine is essential. Here are some ways to do it:

Start and End Your Day with Gratitude: Begin and end each day by reflecting on the things you are grateful for. Use this time to focus on the blessings in your life and express gratitude for them.

Use Positive Affirmations: Use positive affirmations to cultivate a mindset of gratitude. Repeat affirmations such as "I am grateful for the blessings in my life" or "I am thankful for the opportunities that come my way" to stay focused on the positive.

Express Gratitude to Others: Express gratitude to the people in your life who have made a positive impact. Take time to thank them for their contributions and let them know how much you appreciate them.

Practice Random Acts of Kindness: Practice random acts of kindness to cultivate gratitude and give back to others. Look for opportunities to make a positive impact on the world and brighten someone's day.

In conclusion, gratitude is a powerful tool in living a purposeful life. By appreciating the present moment, focusing on what matters, practicing mindfulness, giving back, and keeping a gratitude journal, you can cultivate a mindset of gratitude and find joy in the journey. Remember to incorporate gratitude into your daily routine by starting and ending your day with gratitude, using positive affirmations, expressing gratitude to others, and practicing random acts of kindness. Stay focused on the blessings in your life and live with purpose and gratitude.

Chapter 15: Living a Life of Service to Others

Living a life of service to others is a critical aspect of living a purposeful life. It allows you to use your gifts and talents to make a positive impact on the world and fulfill your purpose. In this chapter, we will explore the importance of living a life of service to others and how to incorporate it into your daily routine.

Identify Your Gifts and Talents: The first step in living a life of service to others is to identify your gifts and talents. Understand what you are good at and how you can use those skills to make a positive impact on the world.

Find Your Passion: Finding your passion is essential in living a life of service to others. Understand what motivates you and what causes you are passionate about. Use this passion to guide your actions and make a difference in the world.

Volunteer Your Time and Resources: Volunteering your time and resources is an excellent way to make a positive impact on the world. Look for opportunities to give back to your community and serve others. Whether it's volunteering at a local charity or donating your resources to those in need, find ways to make a difference.

Use Your Career to Make a Difference: Your career is also an excellent way to make a positive impact on the world. Look for ways to use your skills and expertise to make a difference in your industry and serve others.

Practice Random Acts of Kindness: Small acts of kindness can make a big impact on the world. Practice random acts of kindness, such as paying for someone's coffee or holding the door open for a stranger. These small acts can brighten someone's day and make a positive impact on the world.

Incorporating living a life of service to others into your daily routine is essential. Here are some ways to do it:

Schedule Service Activities: Make service to others a regular part of your life by scheduling regular service activities. Look for opportunities to volunteer your time and resources, and make a commitment to serving others.

Practice Empathy: Empathy is essential in living a life of service to others. Take the time to understand the needs of others and how you can make a positive impact on their lives. Practice empathy by listening to others and putting yourself in their shoes.

Connect with Others: Connecting with others is essential in living a life of service to others. Seek out opportunities to connect with people in your community and build meaningful relationships. Use these connections to identify ways to serve and make a positive impact on the world.

Be Mindful of Your Actions: Be mindful of your actions and how they impact others. Look for ways to make a positive impact on the world through your daily actions, such as being kind to others, using your resources to help those in need, and making ethical decisions in your career.

In conclusion, living a life of service to others is an essential aspect of living a purposeful life. By identifying your gifts and talents, finding your passion, volunteering your time and resources, using your career to make a difference, and practicing random acts of kindness, you can make a positive impact on the world and fulfill your purpose. Remember to incorporate living a life of service to others into your daily routine by scheduling service activities, practicing empathy, connecting with others, and being mindful of your actions. Live with purpose and make a positive impact on the world.

Chapter 16: The Importance of Rest and Self-Care in Pursuing Your Purpose

Rest and self-care are often overlooked in the pursuit of our purpose. However, they are essential in maintaining our physical, emotional, and spiritual well-being, which is critical to fulfilling our purpose. In this chapter, we will explore the importance of rest and self-care in pursuing your purpose and how to incorporate it into your daily routine.

Prioritize Rest: Rest is essential in maintaining our physical and emotional well-being. Prioritize rest by getting enough sleep, taking breaks when you need them, and scheduling downtime in your schedule. Don't underestimate the power of rest in fueling your purpose and allowing you to show up as your best self.

Practice Self-Care: Self-care is essential in maintaining our emotional and spiritual well-being. Take care of yourself by engaging in activities that bring you joy and relaxation. This can include exercise, meditation, spending time with loved ones, or pursuing hobbies that make you happy.

Set Boundaries: Setting boundaries is critical in protecting our well-being and allowing us to pursue our purpose effectively. Learn to say no to activities that drain your energy or do not align with your purpose. Set boundaries around work and personal time to ensure that you have enough time for rest and self-care.

Engage in Activities that Renew Your Energy: Engage in activities that renew your energy and fuel your purpose. This can include spending time in nature, reading inspiring books, or attending events that align with your passions and interests.

Take Care of Your Physical Health: Taking care of your physical health is essential in pursuing your purpose. Make sure that you are eating a healthy diet, getting enough exercise, and taking care of any physical health issues that arise. Your physical health impacts your emotional and spiritual well-being, so prioritize it in your daily routine.

Incorporating rest and self-care into your daily routine is essential. Here are some ways to do it:

Create a Self-Care Routine: Create a self-care routine that aligns with your values and purpose. This can include engaging in activities that bring you joy and relaxation, taking breaks when you need them, and prioritizing rest.

Schedule Rest Time: Schedule rest time into your daily routine to ensure that you are getting enough rest. This can include taking breaks during the workday, setting aside time each day to rest, or scheduling downtime into your weekend.

Practice Mindfulness: Mindfulness is a powerful tool in practicing self-care and rest. Practice mindfulness by staying present in the moment, letting go of distractions, and focusing on the things that matter most.

Connect with Others: Connecting with others is essential in practicing self-care and rest. Seek out opportunities to connect with people who support your well-being and make you feel energized and inspired.

In conclusion, rest and self-care are essential in pursuing your purpose. By prioritizing rest, practicing self-care, setting boundaries, engaging in activities that renew your energy, and taking care of your physical health, you can maintain your physical, emotional, and spiritual well-being and fulfill your purpose. Remember to incorporate rest and self-care into your daily routine by creating a self-care routine, scheduling rest time, practicing mindfulness, and connecting with others. Live with purpose and take care of yourself along the way.

Chapter 17: The Role of Faith in Living a Life of Purpose

Faith plays a significant role in living a life of purpose. It provides a foundation for our beliefs and values, and guides us on our journey towards fulfilling our purpose. In this chapter, we will explore the role of faith in living a life of purpose and how to incorporate it into your daily routine.

Find Your Spiritual Foundation: Finding your spiritual foundation is essential in living a life of purpose. Identify the spiritual practices and beliefs that resonate with you, and use them as a guide on your journey towards fulfilling your purpose.

Seek Guidance and Wisdom: Seek guidance and wisdom from your faith community, spiritual leaders, and religious texts. Use these resources to gain insights into your purpose and how to live a life that aligns with your values and beliefs.

Practice Gratitude and Prayer: Gratitude and prayer are powerful tools in cultivating faith and living a life of purpose. Practice gratitude by focusing on the blessings in your life and expressing thankfulness for them. Practice prayer by connecting with a higher power and seeking guidance on your purpose and life journey.

Live with Integrity and Purpose: Living with integrity and purpose is essential in living a life of faith and fulfilling your purpose. Use your faith as a guide for making ethical decisions and living in alignment with your values and beliefs.

Serve Others: Serving others is a critical aspect of living a life of faith and purpose. Use your gifts and talents to make a positive impact on the world and serve others.

Incorporating faith into your daily routine is essential. Here are some ways to do it:

Practice Daily Devotionals: Practice daily devotionals, such as reading religious texts or reflecting on your spiritual beliefs. This can help you stay connected to your faith and guide your actions and decisions throughout the day.

Attend Religious Services: Attend religious services regularly to connect with your faith community and gain insights into your purpose and life journey.

Join a Faith-Based Community: Join a faith-based community to connect with others who share your beliefs and values. This community can provide support, guidance, and encouragement on your journey towards fulfilling your purpose.

Practice Gratitude and Prayer Daily: Practice gratitude and prayer daily to cultivate your faith and stay connected to your higher power.

In conclusion, faith plays a significant role in living a life of purpose. By finding your spiritual foundation, seeking guidance and wisdom, practicing gratitude and prayer, living with integrity and purpose, and serving others, you can live a life of faith and fulfill your purpose. Remember to incorporate faith into your daily routine by practicing daily devotionals, attending religious services, joining a faith-based community, and practicing gratitude and prayer daily. Live with faith and purpose, and make a positive impact on the world.

Chapter 18: Navigating Relationships and Community in Pursuing Your Purpose

Relationships and community play an important role in pursuing your purpose. They provide support, guidance, and encouragement, and can help you to stay focused on your goals. In this chapter, we will explore how to navigate relationships and community in pursuing your purpose.

Identify Your Support System: Identify the people in your life who support your purpose and well-being. These can include friends, family, mentors, and members of your faith community. Lean on these individuals for support and guidance as you pursue your purpose.

Surround Yourself with Positive Influences: Surround yourself with people who have a positive influence on your life and support your purpose. Seek out individuals who share your values and beliefs, and who inspire and motivate you to be your best self.

Set Boundaries: Setting boundaries is essential in maintaining healthy relationships and staying focused on your purpose. Learn to say no to activities that drain your energy or do not align with your purpose. Set boundaries around work and personal time to ensure that you have enough time to pursue your purpose and engage in self-care.

Communicate Your Purpose: Communicate your purpose to the people in your life. Help them understand what you are working towards and why it is important to you. This can help them to support you and provide guidance and encouragement along the way.

Give Back to Your Community: Giving back to your community is an excellent way to connect with others and make a positive impact on the world. Look for opportunities to serve others and use your gifts and talents to make a difference in your community.

Incorporating relationships and community into your daily routine is essential. Here are some ways to do it:

Schedule Time for Relationships: Schedule time for relationships into your daily routine. Whether it's spending time with loved ones or connecting with your faith community, make sure that you prioritize these relationships and give them the time they deserve.

Seek Out Mentors and Role Models: Seek out mentors and role models who can provide guidance and support on your journey towards fulfilling your purpose. These individuals can help you to stay focused on your goals and provide insight into how to achieve them.

Join a Group or Organization: Join a group or organization that aligns with your purpose and interests. This can provide opportunities to connect with like-minded individuals and make a positive impact on the world.

Attend Networking Events: Attend networking events to connect with individuals who can help you to achieve your goals and support your purpose. These events can provide opportunities to meet new people and gain insight into your industry or field.

In conclusion, relationships and community are essential in pursuing your purpose. By identifying your support system, surrounding yourself with positive influences, setting boundaries, communicating your purpose, and giving back to your community, you can navigate relationships and community effectively and fulfill your purpose. Remember to incorporate relationships and community into your daily routine by scheduling time for relationships, seeking out mentors and role models, joining a group or organization, and attending networking events. Live with purpose and make meaningful connections along the way.

Chapter 19: The Role of Perseverance in Achieving Your Purpose

Perseverance is essential in achieving your purpose. It allows you to overcome obstacles, setbacks, and challenges, and stay focused on your goals. In this chapter, we will explore the role of perseverance in achieving your purpose and how to cultivate it in your life.

Define Your Purpose: Defining your purpose is essential in cultivating perseverance. Understand what you are working towards and why it is important to you. This clarity can help you stay focused and motivated in the face of challenges.

Set Realistic Goals: Setting realistic goals is critical in achieving your purpose. Break down your purpose into smaller, achievable goals, and work towards them one step at a time. This can help you to stay motivated and focused on the bigger picture.

Embrace Failure: Failure is a natural part of the journey towards achieving your purpose. Embrace failure as an opportunity to learn and grow, and use it as a stepping stone towards success.

Develop a Resilient Mindset: Developing a resilient mindset is essential in cultivating perseverance. Learn to bounce back from setbacks and challenges and use them as opportunities to grow and learn.

Stay Focused on Your Purpose: Staying focused on your purpose is essential in cultivating perseverance. Use your purpose as a guide for making decisions and taking action towards achieving your goals.

Incorporating perseverance into your daily routine is essential. Here are some ways to do it:

Cultivate a Growth Mindset: Cultivate a growth mindset by believing in your ability to learn and grow from challenges and setbacks. This can help you to stay motivated and focused on your purpose.

Stay Consistent: Consistency is critical in achieving your purpose. Stay consistent in your actions and goals, and make progress towards your purpose every day.

Seek Support: Seek support from your support system, mentors, and role models. These individuals can provide guidance, support, and encouragement as you pursue your purpose.

Practice Self-Care: Practicing self-care is essential in cultivating perseverance. Take care of yourself by engaging in activities that bring you joy and relaxation, and prioritize rest and self-care.

In conclusion, perseverance is essential in achieving your purpose. By defining your purpose, setting realistic goals, embracing failure, developing a resilient mindset, and staying focused on your purpose, you can cultivate perseverance and achieve your goals. Remember to incorporate perseverance into your daily routine by cultivating a growth mindset, staying consistent, seeking support, and practicing self-care. Live with purpose and cultivate perseverance along the way.

Chapter 20: Discovering Your Life's Mission and Calling

Discovering your life's mission and calling is a critical step in living a purposeful life. It involves understanding your unique gifts and talents, identifying the needs of the world, and finding the intersection between the two. In this chapter, we will explore how to discover your life's mission and calling.

Identify Your Unique Gifts and Talents: Identifying your unique gifts and talents is essential in discovering your life's mission and calling. Reflect on the things that you are good at and passionate about, and consider how you can use these skills to make a positive impact on the world.

Identify the Needs of the World: Identifying the needs of the world is critical in discovering your life's mission and calling. Look at the problems and challenges that exist in the world and consider how you can use your gifts and talents to address them.

Find the Intersection: Finding the intersection between your unique gifts and talents and the needs of the world is where your life's mission and calling lies. Consider how you can use your skills and passions to make a positive impact on the world.

Explore Your Passions: Exploring your passions is essential in discovering your life's mission and calling. Consider the things that bring you joy and fulfillment, and how you can use these passions to make a positive impact on the world.

Seek Guidance: Seeking guidance from mentors, coaches, and spiritual leaders can provide insight into discovering your life's mission and calling. These individuals can help you to gain clarity and direction on your purpose and life journey.

Incorporating the discovery of your life's mission and calling into your daily routine is essential. Here are some ways to do it:

Engage in Self-Reflection: Engage in self-reflection by taking time to reflect on your unique gifts and talents, passions, and the needs of the world. This can help you gain insight into your life's mission and calling.

Explore Opportunities: Explore opportunities to use your gifts and talents to make a positive impact on the world. Look for ways to serve others and engage in activities that align with your passions and interests.

Connect with Like-Minded Individuals: Connect with like-minded individuals who share your values and passions. This community can provide support, guidance, and inspiration as you discover your life's mission and calling.

Practice Mindfulness: Practice mindfulness by staying present in the moment and focusing on the things that matter most. This can help you to gain clarity and direction on your purpose and life journey.

In conclusion, discovering your life's mission and calling is a critical step in living a purposeful life. By identifying your unique gifts and talents, identifying the needs of the world, finding the intersection between the two, exploring your passions, and seeking guidance, you can discover your life's mission and calling. Remember to incorporate the discovery of your life's mission and calling into your daily routine by engaging in self-reflection, exploring opportunities, connecting with like-minded individuals, and practicing mindfulness. Live with purpose and fulfill your life's mission and calling.

Chapter 21: The Importance of Character in Living a Purposeful Life

Character is an essential aspect of living a purposeful life. It involves developing qualities such as integrity, honesty, and compassion, and using them as a guide for making decisions and taking actions towards fulfilling your purpose. In this chapter, we will explore the importance of character in living a purposeful life and how to develop it.

Define Your Values: Defining your values is essential in developing your character. Identify the qualities that are most important to you, such as honesty, integrity, and compassion, and use them as a guide for making decisions and taking action towards fulfilling your purpose.

Practice Self-Awareness: Practicing self-awareness is critical in developing your character. Be aware of your thoughts, feelings, and actions, and how they impact yourself and others. Use this awareness to cultivate qualities such as empathy and compassion.

Cultivate Resilience: Cultivating resilience is essential in developing your character. Learn to bounce back from setbacks and challenges and use them as opportunities to grow and learn. This resilience can help you to stay focused and motivated in the face of obstacles.

Practice Gratitude: Practicing gratitude is a powerful way to develop your character. Focus on the blessings in your life and express gratitude for them. This can help you to cultivate qualities such as humility and appreciation.

Serve Others: Serving others is a critical aspect of developing your character. Use your gifts and talents to make a positive impact on the world and serve others. This service can help you to cultivate qualities such as empathy and compassion.

Incorporating character development into your daily routine is essential. Here are some ways to do it:

Set Character-Based Goals: Set goals that are based on character development, such as cultivating empathy or practicing gratitude. Use these goals as a guide for making decisions and taking action towards fulfilling your purpose.

Practice Self-Reflection: Practice self-reflection by taking time to reflect on your thoughts, feelings, and actions, and how they align with your values and character. Use this reflection to cultivate qualities such as self-awareness and humility.

Seek Feedback: Seek feedback from others on your character and how you can improve. This feedback can provide valuable insights into your character development and help you to grow and learn.

Connect with Like-Minded Individuals: Connect with like-minded individuals who share your values and character traits. This community can provide support, guidance, and encouragement as you develop your character.

In conclusion, character is an essential aspect of living a purposeful life. By defining your values, practicing self-awareness, cultivating resilience, practicing gratitude, and serving others, you can develop your character and use it as a guide for making decisions and taking action towards fulfilling your purpose. Remember to incorporate character development into your daily routine by setting character-based goals, practicing self-reflection, seeking feedback, and connecting with like-minded individuals. Live with purpose and cultivate your character along the way.

Chapter 22: Overcoming Distractions and Staying Focused on Your Purpose

Distractions can make it challenging to stay focused on your purpose. They can take you away from what is essential and cause you to lose sight of your goals. In this chapter, we will explore how to overcome distractions and stay focused on your purpose.

Define Your Purpose: Defining your purpose is critical in staying focused on your goals. Understand what you are working towards and why it is essential to you. This clarity can help you to stay motivated and focused in the face of distractions.

Identify Your Distractions: Identifying your distractions is essential in overcoming them. Consider the things that take you away from your purpose, such as social media or television, and develop strategies to manage them.

Set Boundaries: Setting boundaries is critical in staying focused on your purpose. Learn to say no to activities that do not align with your purpose, and set boundaries around work and personal time to ensure that you have enough time to pursue your purpose and engage in self-care.

Create a Plan: Creating a plan is essential in staying focused on your purpose. Break down your purpose into smaller, achievable goals, and develop a plan to achieve them. Use this plan as a guide for making decisions and taking action towards your goals.

Use Visualization: Visualization is a powerful tool in staying focused on your purpose. Visualize yourself achieving your goals and living a purposeful life. This can help you to stay motivated and focused on your purpose.

Incorporating strategies to overcome distractions into your daily routine is essential. Here are some ways to do it:

Practice Mindfulness: Practice mindfulness by staying present in the moment and focusing on the things that matter most. This can help you to avoid distractions and stay focused on your purpose.

Manage Your Time: Manage your time effectively by setting priorities and using your time wisely. Avoid multitasking and focus on one task at a time to stay focused and productive.

Minimize Distractions: Minimize distractions by removing them from your environment. Turn off notifications on your phone, limit your time on social media, and create a distraction-free workspace.

Seek Support: Seek support from your support system, mentors, and role models. These individuals can provide guidance, support, and encouragement as you pursue your purpose and stay focused on your goals.

In conclusion, overcoming distractions and staying focused on your purpose is critical in living a purposeful life. By defining your purpose, identifying your distractions, setting boundaries, creating a plan, and using visualization, you can overcome distractions and stay focused on your goals. Remember to incorporate strategies to overcome distractions into your daily routine by practicing mindfulness, managing your time, minimizing distractions, and seeking support. Live with purpose and stay focused on your goals along the way.

Chapter 23: Building a Support System for Pursuing Your Purpose

Building a support system is essential in pursuing your purpose. It involves surrounding yourself with individuals who believe in you, support your goals, and provide guidance and encouragement along the way. In this chapter, we will explore how to build a support system for pursuing your purpose.

Identify Your Needs: Identifying your needs is critical in building a support system. Consider the areas where you need support, such as emotional support or guidance, and use these needs as a guide for building your support system.

Seek Out Like-Minded Individuals: Seeking out like-minded individuals who share your values and passions can provide valuable support and encouragement. Look for individuals who are pursuing similar goals and share similar interests and values.

Build Relationships with Mentors and Role Models: Building relationships with mentors and role models can provide guidance and support as you pursue your purpose. These individuals can provide valuable insights and advice on achieving your goals.

Connect with a Community: Connecting with a community can provide a sense of belonging and support as you pursue your purpose. Consider joining groups or organizations that align with your values and interests.

Communicate Your Goals: Communicating your goals to your support system is critical in building a support system. Share your goals and aspirations with those who support you, and use their feedback and advice to make progress towards your purpose.

Incorporating building a support system into your daily routine is essential. Here are some ways to do it:

Attend Networking Events: Attend networking events and conferences to connect with like-minded individuals and build relationships with mentors and role models.

Join a Support Group: Join a support group to connect with individuals who are pursuing similar goals and share similar interests and values.

Seek Feedback: Seek feedback from your support system on your progress towards your purpose. This feedback can provide valuable insights and advice on achieving your goals.

Schedule Regular Check-Ins: Schedule regular check-ins with your support system to stay connected and accountable in pursuing your purpose.

In conclusion, building a support system is essential in pursuing your purpose. By identifying your needs, seeking out like-minded individuals, building relationships with mentors and role models, connecting with a community, and communicating your goals, you can build a support system that provides guidance, support, and encouragement as you pursue your purpose. Remember to incorporate building a support system into your daily routine by attending networking events, joining a support group, seeking feedback, and scheduling regular check-ins. Live with purpose and build a support system that helps you achieve your goals.

Chapter 24: Embracing Change and Adaptability on Your Life Journey

Change is inevitable in life, and learning to adapt to change is critical in living a purposeful life. It involves being flexible, open-minded, and resilient, and using change as an opportunity for growth and learning. In this chapter, we will explore how to embrace change and adaptability on your life journey.

Accept the Reality of Change: Accepting the reality of change is critical in embracing it. Understand that change is a natural part of life and that it can provide opportunities for growth and learning.

Cultivate Resilience: Cultivating resilience is essential in adapting to change. Learn to bounce back from setbacks and challenges and use them as opportunities to grow and learn. This resilience can help you to stay focused and motivated in the face of change.

Practice Flexibility: Practicing flexibility is critical in adapting to change. Be open-minded and willing to adjust your plans and goals as needed to accommodate changes in your life journey.

Embrace Learning: Embracing learning is essential in adapting to change. Use change as an opportunity to learn new skills and gain new experiences. This can help you to grow and evolve as a person.

Seek Support: Seeking support from your support system can provide guidance and encouragement as you adapt to change. These individuals can provide valuable insights and advice on navigating change.

Incorporating adaptability into your daily routine is essential. Here are some ways to do it:

Practice Mindfulness: Practice mindfulness by staying present in the moment and focusing on the things that matter most. This can help you to stay focused and adaptable in the face of change.

Stay Positive: Stay positive and optimistic in the face of change. Use positive self-talk and focus on the opportunities that change can provide.

Reflect on Your Experiences: Reflect on your experiences and what you have learned from them. Use this reflection to cultivate resilience and adaptability.

Set Realistic Expectations: Set realistic expectations for yourself and others in the face of change. Understand that change takes time and that adaptation is a process.

In conclusion, embracing change and adaptability is critical in living a purposeful life. By accepting the reality of change, cultivating resilience, practicing flexibility, embracing learning, and seeking support, you can adapt to change and use it as an opportunity for growth and learning. Remember to incorporate adaptability into your daily routine by practicing mindfulness, staying positive, reflecting on your experiences, and setting realistic expectations. Live with purpose and embrace change along the way.

Chapter 25: Learning from Failures and Mistakes on Your Purposeful Path

Failure and mistakes are a natural part of life, and learning from them is critical in living a purposeful life. It involves using these experiences as opportunities for growth and learning, and developing resilience and perseverance in the face of challenges. In this chapter, we will explore how to learn from failures and mistakes on your purposeful path.

Embrace Failure: Embracing failure is critical in learning from it. Understand that failure is a natural part of life and that it can provide valuable insights and opportunities for growth and learning.

Practice Self-Compassion: Practicing self-compassion is essential in learning from failures and mistakes. Be kind and understanding towards yourself and use these experiences as opportunities for growth and learning, rather than dwelling on them negatively.

Analyze Your Mistakes: Analyzing your mistakes is critical in learning from them. Understand what went wrong and how you can improve, and use this knowledge to prevent similar mistakes in the future.

Cultivate Resilience: Cultivating resilience is essential in learning from failures and mistakes. Learn to bounce back from setbacks and challenges and use them as opportunities to grow and learn. This resilience can help you to stay focused and motivated in the face of challenges.

Seek Feedback: Seeking feedback from others on your failures and mistakes can provide valuable insights and advice on how to improve. Use this feedback to learn and grow from these experiences.

Incorporating learning from failures and mistakes into your daily routine is essential. Here are some ways to do it:

Practice Reflection: Practice reflection by taking time to reflect on your failures and mistakes, and what you have learned from them. Use this reflection to cultivate resilience and perseverance.

Set Goals: Set goals that are based on your learning from failures and mistakes, such as improving your communication skills or time management. Use these goals as a guide for making decisions and taking action towards your purpose.

Celebrate Small Wins: Celebrate small wins along the way, even if they are minor. These wins can help you to stay motivated and focused on your purpose.

Seek Support: Seek support from your support system as you learn from failures and mistakes. These individuals can provide guidance, support, and encouragement as you grow and learn.

In conclusion, learning from failures and mistakes is critical in living a purposeful life. By embracing failure, practicing self-compassion, analyzing your mistakes, cultivating resilience, and seeking feedback, you can learn and grow from these experiences. Remember to incorporate learning from failures and mistakes into your daily routine by practicing reflection, setting goals, celebrating small wins, and seeking support. Live with purpose and learn from failures and mistakes along the way.

Chapter 26: Aligning Your Goals with God's Purpose for Your Life

Aligning your goals with God's purpose for your life is critical in living a purposeful life. It involves seeking God's guidance, understanding His plan for your life, and aligning your goals and actions with His will. In this chapter, we will explore how to align your goals with God's purpose for your life.

Seek God's Guidance: Seeking God's guidance is essential in aligning your goals with His purpose for your life. Pray and seek His wisdom and guidance on your life journey.

Study His Word: Studying His word can provide insight into His plan for your life and guidance on aligning your goals and actions with His will.

Live in Obedience: Living in obedience to God's will is critical in aligning your goals with His purpose for your life. Seek to honor and obey Him in all areas of your life, including your goals and actions.

Listen to His Voice: Listening to His voice can provide direction and guidance on aligning your goals with His will. Be open to His leading and guidance on your life journey.

Surrender Your Plans: Surrendering your plans to God is critical in aligning your goals with His purpose for your life. Trust in His plan for your life and be willing to adjust your goals and actions as needed to align with His will.

Incorporating aligning your goals with God's purpose into your daily routine is essential. Here are some ways to do it:

Start and End Your Day with Prayer: Start and end your day with prayer to seek God's guidance and wisdom on your life journey.

Meditate on His Word: Meditate on His word and seek guidance on aligning your goals and actions with His will.

Practice Gratitude: Practice gratitude for God's blessings in your life and seek to honor and obey Him in all areas of your life.

Connect with a Spiritual Community: Connect with a spiritual community to gain support, guidance, and encouragement in aligning your goals with God's purpose for your life.

In conclusion, aligning your goals with God's purpose for your life is critical in living a purposeful life. By seeking God's guidance, studying His word, living in obedience, listening to His voice, and surrendering your plans, you can align your goals and actions with His will. Remember to incorporate aligning your goals with God's purpose into your daily routine by starting and ending your day with prayer, meditating on His word, practicing gratitude, and connecting with a spiritual community. Live with purpose and align your goals with God's purpose for your life along the way.

Chapter 27: The Role of Wisdom in Living a Purposeful Life

Wisdom is critical in living a purposeful life. It involves seeking knowledge and understanding, making wise decisions, and using discernment in all areas of your life. In this chapter, we will explore the role of wisdom in living a purposeful life.

Seek Knowledge and Understanding: Seeking knowledge and understanding is essential in living a purposeful life. Learn and grow in all areas of your life, including spiritually, emotionally, and intellectually.

Make Wise Decisions: Making wise decisions is critical in living a purposeful life. Use discernment and seek God's guidance in making decisions that align with your purpose.

Use Discernment: Using discernment is essential in living a purposeful life. Seek to understand the truth and use this understanding to make wise decisions.

Practice Self-Control: Practicing self-control is critical in living a purposeful life. Exercise self-control in all areas of your life, including your thoughts, emotions, and actions.

Embrace Humility: Embracing humility is essential in living a purposeful life. Seek to understand and acknowledge your limitations and weaknesses, and use this understanding to grow and learn.

Incorporating wisdom into your daily routine is essential. Here are some ways to do it:

Study God's Word: Study God's word and seek wisdom and understanding from His teachings.

Practice Reflection: Practice reflection on your decisions and actions, and seek to learn and grow from your experiences.

Seek Wise Counsel: Seek wise counsel from mentors and role models who can provide guidance and advice on living a purposeful life.

Cultivate Patience: Cultivate patience in all areas of your life, and seek to understand that wisdom takes time and practice.

In conclusion, wisdom is critical in living a purposeful life. By seeking knowledge and understanding, making wise decisions, using discernment, practicing self-control, and embracing humility, you can live with purpose and intention. Remember to incorporate wisdom into your daily routine by studying God's word, practicing reflection, seeking wise counsel, and cultivating patience. Live with purpose and wisdom along the way.

Chapter 28: Building a Legacy of Purpose and Impact

Building a legacy of purpose and impact is essential in living a purposeful life. It involves using your gifts and talents to make a positive impact on the world around you, and leaving a lasting legacy for future generations. In this chapter, we will explore how to build a legacy of purpose and impact.

Identify Your Gifts and Talents: Identifying your gifts and talents is critical in building a legacy of purpose and impact. Understand what you are passionate about and what you do well, and use these strengths to make a positive impact.

Set Goals: Setting goals is essential in building a legacy of purpose and impact. Create a vision for your life and set specific goals that align with this vision.

Develop a Plan: Developing a plan is critical in building a legacy of purpose and impact. Create a plan that outlines the steps you need to take to achieve your goals and make a positive impact.

Take Action: Taking action is essential in building a legacy of purpose and impact. Take intentional steps towards your goals and use your gifts and talents to make a positive impact on the world around you.

Leave a Legacy: Leaving a legacy is critical in building a legacy of purpose and impact. Use your life to make a lasting impact on future generations, and create a legacy that reflects your purpose and values.

Incorporating building a legacy of purpose and impact into your daily routine is essential. Here are some ways to do it:

Live with Intention: Live with intention and purpose in all areas of your life, and seek to make a positive impact on the world around you.

Practice Generosity: Practice generosity in all areas of your life, including your time, talents, and resources. Use your gifts to make a positive impact on others.

Seek Opportunities: Seek opportunities to make a positive impact on the world around you, including volunteering, mentoring, and serving others.

Connect with a Community: Connect with a community of like-minded individuals who share your values and passion for making a positive impact on the world.

In conclusion, building a legacy of purpose and impact is essential in living a purposeful life. By identifying your gifts and talents, setting goals, developing a plan, taking action, and leaving a legacy, you can use your life to make a positive impact on the world around you. Remember to incorporate building a legacy of purpose and impact into your daily routine by living with intention, practicing generosity, seeking opportunities, and connecting with a community. Live with purpose and build a legacy of purpose and impact along the way.

Chapter 29: Living with Joy and Purpose in Every Season of Life

Living with joy and purpose in every season of life is essential in living a fulfilling and purposeful life. It involves finding meaning and purpose in every stage of life, and embracing each season with gratitude and joy. In this chapter, we will explore how to live with joy and purpose in every season of life.

Embrace Each Season: Embracing each season of life is critical in living with joy and purpose. Understand that each season of life brings unique challenges and opportunities, and embrace each one with gratitude and joy.

Find Meaning and Purpose: Finding meaning and purpose in every stage of life is essential in living with joy and purpose. Seek to understand the purpose of each season and find ways to make a positive impact on the world around you.

Cultivate Gratitude: Cultivating gratitude is critical in living with joy and purpose in every season of life. Focus on the blessings in your life and seek to find joy and gratitude in all situations.

Stay Connected: Staying connected with loved ones and your community is essential in living with joy and purpose in every season of life. Build meaningful relationships and seek support and guidance from those around you.

Practice Self-Care: Practicing self-care is critical in living with joy and purpose in every season of life. Take care of your physical, emotional, and spiritual health, and prioritize activities that bring you joy and fulfillment.

Incorporating living with joy and purpose in every season of life into your daily routine is essential. Here are some ways to do it:

Practice Mindfulness: Practice mindfulness by being present in each moment and seeking joy and gratitude in all situations.

Set Goals: Set goals that align with your purpose and values, and take intentional steps towards achieving them in every season of life.

Connect with a Community: Connect with a community of individuals who share your values and passion for living with joy and purpose in every season of life.

Celebrate Milestones: Celebrate milestones in every season of life, no matter how small they may seem. These celebrations can help you to stay motivated and focused on your purpose.

In conclusion, living with joy and purpose in every season of life is critical in living a fulfilling and purposeful life. By embracing each season, finding meaning and purpose, cultivating gratitude, staying connected, and practicing self-care, you can live with joy and purpose in every stage of life. Remember to incorporate living with joy and purpose in every season of life into your daily routine by practicing mindfulness, setting goals, connecting with a community, and celebrating milestones. Live with purpose and joy in every season of life.

Chapter 30: Conclusion - Embracing God's Plan for Your Life

Embracing God's plan for your life is critical in living a purposeful life. It involves seeking His guidance, understanding His will for your life, and aligning your goals and actions with His purpose. In this chapter, we will summarize the key points and explore the importance of embracing God's plan for your life.

Living a life of purpose is about seeking God's guidance and understanding His plan for your life. It involves discovering your spiritual gifts, finding your passion and purpose, developing a vision for your life, and aligning your goals with His purpose. Along the way, you may encounter setbacks, obstacles, and doubts, but by trusting in God's guidance and persevering, you can overcome these challenges and live with courage and conviction.

To live a purposeful life, you must also cultivate wisdom, embrace each season of life, and build a legacy of purpose and impact. By seeking knowledge and understanding, making wise decisions, using discernment, practicing self-control, and embracing humility, you can live with purpose and intention. Embracing each season of life with gratitude and joy, staying connected with loved ones and your community, and practicing self-care are essential in living a fulfilling life. Building a legacy of purpose and impact is about using your gifts and talents to make a positive impact on the world and leaving a lasting legacy for future generations.

In conclusion, embracing God's plan for your life is critical in living a purposeful life. Seek His guidance, understand His will for your life, and align your goals and actions with His purpose. Cultivate wisdom, embrace each season of life, and build a legacy of purpose and impact. Remember to live with gratitude, joy, and intention in all areas of your life. By living with purpose and embracing God's plan for your life, you can make a positive impact on the world and leave a lasting legacy for future generations.

Also by Dorothy Vincent

The Case of the Missing Heirloom: A Whodunit Mystery
The Lost City of Atlantis: A Young Adult Adventure
Living Authentically: Embracing Your Unique Identity
The Faithful Witness: Conviction and Courage in Uncertain Times
Breaking the Mold: Shattering Expectations and Chasing Dreams
The Art of Being Yourself: Uncovering the Power of Authenticity
Living a Life of Purpose: Discovering God's Plan for Your Life

About the Publisher

Accepting manuscripts in the most categories. We love to help people get their words available to the world.

Revival Waves of Glory focus is to provide more options to be published. We do traditional paperbacks, hardcovers, audio books and ebooks all over the world. A traditional royalty-based publisher that offers self-publishing options, Revival Waves provides a very author friendly and transparent publishing process, with President Bill Vincent involved in the full process of your book. Send us your manuscript and we will contact you as soon as possible.

Contact: Bill Vincent at rwgpublishing@yahoo.com

www.ingramcontent.com/pod-product-compliance
Lightning Source LLC
LaVergne TN
LVHW042000060526
838200LV00041B/1800